DRIFT

DRIFT

poems by **Mary Kinzie**

 ALFRED A. KNOPF   NEW YORK   2003

THIS IS A BORZOI BOOK
PUBLISHED BY ALFRED A. KNOPF

Published in the United States by Alfred A. Knopf,
a division of Random House, Inc., New York,
and simultaneously in Canada by Random House
of Canada Limited, Toronto.
Distributed by Random House, Inc., New York.

www.randomhouse.com/knopf/poetry

Knopf, Borzoi Books, and the colophon are registered trademarks of
Random House, Inc.
The suite of poems "Book of Tears" has appeared in *Graven Images: Studies in Law,
Culture and the Sacred*, an annual journal edited by Sonja Hansard-Weiner and Andrew
Weiner (University of Wisconsin–Madison, 2002). "After Frost at Midnight" and "Zeno at
Zero" were published in *Slate*. "Air Shaft" appeared in *The New Yorker*. "After
Frost at Midnight," "Midwinter," and *"Objet"* have also appeared in
A Poet's Guide to Poetry (University of Chicago, 1999).

Library of Congress Cataloging-in-Publication Data
Kinzie, Mary.
Drift : poems / by Mary Kinzie.—1st ed.
p.   cm.
ISBN 0-375-41463-0
I. Title.
PS3561.I59 D74 2003
811'.54—dc21
2002069427
Manufactured in the United States of America
First Edition

For my daughter

Contents

~

D R I F T

Hour on Hour

Easy to say

Hard to look out
across all the minutes
crawling
in their sameness
as a planet drags the atoms
making a slight curve where
the buildings stop them
killing time

Dust is time
gravel in the alley
time
loosely grinding
like dice in a cup
shapes that darken
but do not save
loom out of time
with a spattering
of terrible song

Daughters
my sister and I
move our heads
and blink
as if the empty moment
with a watery
low warble
would ever break

hit about
coating with coolness

We have not learned
to sing the notes
of our kind
but know
them from the rest
catch them uncertain
above us
like threads
of light

So dry so long here
on the rough paving
our wings
stick fast to a pole
knobby with flies
someone put in our nest
to pull
all of us out

Airless
under the glare
beside us fall
hot colored flies
on the trash from the bins
bits of hours?
pieces of thirst!
            sparks
of unchange

Farm

Hard gray dirt
in the day
leaves soft
with dust
      at night
black florets
of mildew fume
from any cloth
lain upon
spider fashion

        If it's dry you
           worry
        If it's wet you
           starve

Far away the blue
square of a discarded
plastic pool
or tarp

I am too young to leave
or to come
in out of the sun
I worry   I starve
I can't think a different thought
but what the day
shoves as it breaks
into my hands
or lays upon the mind
as its denoted
weight still

scalding
from the sparks
at the summer stars'
late centers
seed-cast on the oil
of each midnight
yet wild
up and away
like minnows
at the thought

If it's wet

If it's dry

Flecks dart
from each other
fourmillantes
      fret
down the sides
the legs
up the scalp and
in every breath
heavier   crawl
through the stunned
toil into distance
where pours no power
no sign
only puffs of headlamps
burning

Ropework

Loose cord
along the galvanized downspout
indefinite flail
rings out a summons
as if across a border where
a clockwork village
lives off by itself
(scurry; distant
daylong effort)
tempting one to raise the head
echo of something in A-flat
worry at sea

Porcelain curl by which the teacup
held itself up in the hand
rubbed by fingers
then not
across the glaze pensive
a bit in the powdery key of B

From far off
all the thin ringing
almost inaudible
(not enough shape
for melody)
broken work
from shovels of iron
clanging against the polished clay
of the ditch   *chimmee*
from thin machines
that lift in our absence
phantom receivers to

a phantom voice
from chimes that say this food
or night of sleep is
finished you must waken
you must act with the eye
you must move
the hand quickly
you must die   these
these were as nothing
to the starlike
blinking way
rocking in the air
my body would receive
and orient itself
to the circulating bell
buzzer from the school
the call glowing in my breast
bone as it sank
like a satellite
upon its wavesource
orbiting above where
she was
across the map
of barely breathing
where she was not

Now to cast my thinking
toward the school for larger children
walled like medieval Paris with its
throngs of spires, passages
thrown out in jigsaws
days of low scuffling

bodies jostling on the stairs
is to see girls
pulled into darkened corners
by the men who
stream in and out of the tenements
watchful, intuitive
unfazed by teachers
dulled by waiting
haunted by knives

Scrape thwack
clangor in high wind
and I realize that I *have been*
hearing this
whatever it is
almost music
for weeks in bits
that might link
pattern to loveliness
if only the world
could latch on to the
cables of bast or plastic
the bowlines guys snotters
vangs halyards
the hawsers on their sheaves smoking
whomp   lashing   *kuhCHING*
ringing out   *chimmee*

(Better not reach out
it would cut right through
your life)

For weeks this sound of
ropework
loose from the hand or round
where the hand coiled it
in a ready heap
had been making me almost
happy
      as if the house
of apartments were
being sped by a quirt
to gallop off
through the cool blue days
and long parades of drizzle
into which as yet only a leaf
or two had fallen

Then drowned out
and woven over
it disappeared beyond the
high keen
of elephantine
scouring trucks that reeked
through the alleys
        small in the haze
of their heaving   it
would reform
in waves of dust
until it flagged
noon rusted   then
pocked by the barks
of something crazy

and shiftless set off
by the bands
of neighborhood children
by turns innocent and nasty
(but also nasty-wild)
taunting each other or a bird
that dragged one side

Weary of its failing
energy they fan away
in all directions
leaving in the small
clear silence
a bellnote
high and tender and as in dreams
I seem to see it
off by itself or
see the thought of it
like dead vine
on a robust corrugated tree
up which new vine is
picking a trail
fastening the dry veins
of decay to the tree in the dim,
the glaucous under-
water summer
light
      the vine leaves perhaps
      speckled with fleshy stems
      that seep
      when broken

Is this the light of the time
I no longer live in
               childhood
boredom
through long hours
refractory
with a shadowed glint
waiting for rain
unclear about words
never getting the point
of the joke
is the empty
ringing of not understanding
it like
the strange emerging
shape of the leaf with
the papery fringe at the bud
flapping about
that makes it seem
like ringing
             or like one
repeated note
of pale fine light
poured through its
thin rhythm
of diffusion
upon that man who
sits in a chair   observing
a crack in the ceiling
in the hive of avenues
the shape of this wandering
becoming

definite   errant
tendril of
brown heat
reaching far off
through the plaster
so he has to lean back
to face it
in the small hours
in the old red chair

Still it continues
sound
word
idea
the strange emerging
reflection shaped
to the leaf with the papery
fringe at the bud
loose curling and a
crazed look echoed by
the uneven leaf-lobes or horns
like the devil in Dürer or
goats with knobs of
keratin oddly curled or
broken like the junkyards
they pick shrill
crackling morsels out of
butting about so their genitals
quiver and gashing with
their tiny filthy hooves
or even biting deep into the thigh
with fierce flat yellow teeth

held in a small
jaw cup
innocent nasty goats
on the ash heap
where I live
off by myself
twisting from the rope
of the daylight
waiting for my child

Poet on Small Hillside

Off to myself
unbright
filmed over
with damp like wood
unfit for fire

Sweat thrusting up
under my hair in heavy beads
that burst almost as might
a sore

When the hand
tests the scalp
only a slickness, like the
inside
skin of a plum

Is this pleasant
or a kind of condemnation
such resemblance
fixation
basting

Heat heat
at the rim
of the liable body
                    the sky a net
too tight to swim through
chasing the fish in

Locusts in trees—
heatbites—

veins
large on a hand
that has lifted and written of
flowers autumnal and ancient
hard in color and tough
in bloom—

            yarrow
            helenium

Reeking and swift
the jet stream
of decay
though here in the region
of old age
rags of consciousness
dally like flame
and I
an old man
in a poor suit among thistles
smiling ajitter

Silverprint

—BY HARRY CALLAHAN

Hollow
troughing
in the sand
hurry of wanderer
or camel train
minute
with pattern
as if what
once moved through
were many
and confused

Something
in the distance
feels of
technique
some flat
early
photoactive
airy mass
frowning darker
far away
as it burned

Offoco

exists
because an unfledged lictor
in the long echoing
bowel of stone
could force against the teeth
of some strong person
a cup she could not refuse

Why else should there be
a Roman word
to put toward the mouth
with the notion of force
unless someone   many
had been made to drink
until livid
jiggers of lead

Dawn Swim

This was to have been the summer
concentrated on the new
skill the late-acquiring fingers
gained frivoling over the keys
with Kabalevsky
    a craving came
    to own a harpsichord
    checked like parquet

of running so the hinges of the leg
shone as they struck the ground
to bring a shock against
a whole contiguous
tightening of bone
    clothing
    would hang liquid
    on this frame

a summer when life pushed
acquaintance to the height
of those long passages à clef
in Proust or to the
fever's source
in Friedrich Hölderlin.

Oh and there was lake water
to dip far into with the long
wick of the torso and
pale flare
of arms at the surface
scuffing up a little heat

It got so
far, this notion of a daily
plunge, I thought
    with a pencil
    lifted from the hollow
    gallery of images, particolored
    window chinks that flashed
    strong deeps of liquid
    coiling with gloom
yes I
thought a wetsuit
might be needed to coat
the chilly flesh as morning
in and morning out
I lowered the shark
black thighs into the very
mercury
of morning

Then life drew in

All the distant
people, barely or never
met or long since lost
track of, had either died
after a third procedure or
wrecked their being
with a car
on the way to school
or fought the

ineluctable
        people
worn down to the same nub
forgetful now of all their
little fancies
kinsmen
grown huge as hosts
to node and filament and ditch
filament and node and gash
and thirst and precipice and ditch
which made them
quaking
stare
down the crumpling passage
of their memory where
eye level
water began to brim
slippery pink
at the foot of the bed

Air Shaft

One might find
a little window
even if there were
no sky

There may be air
though dank
sunk
at the base
of an air shaft
booming with cries

One might clear
the surface of grit
so that a small page
could lie there with a pen
and the weevil
with graphite wings

Firebrat

Ghosts of the cats
in the empty
burned apartment
drifting
with the flakes of char
and unbreathable smell

In the basement
under the half inch
of fiberglass
on the boiler
when you press
with the hand a
stammering web
of vermin

Crusted
quick
fleshy

Haired as
warts are and
their feet
heat-hardened

thermobia
domestica

The heat-livened

The fire within

Theine

If compelled
to give it up
I would lift
as leaves do
loosened
from the tree
and feel the floating
thread of my thought
blown out
beyond itself
      line loose
      on the water
wandering
cinder
sleepier
than air

Midwinter

We seem to be dining
yet the salver offers
only the unstirred flame
of the candle whose wax
melts over my fist

Beyond the cloth the gloom
hardens the air
on which a tired head
might strike and
reawaken

     By day
a patch of snow in the yard
flares out
        green gravel, green
          grave O
oh as if a lump of radium
were sending its dolor
into the material darkness

Close Path

What have I trained for   what
have the years of
whatever I did
during them
made me
ready to take on
if the tears are to
stream coldly
like long streaks
of rain down the light
brick of the storehouse
and I become
afraid to look
lest the pain
travel
with my breathing
its path
near enough
to disappear
down

Evening at Morning

Then am I a tear
evaporating
on a plate

Book of Tears

Blue Iris

The world is touched and stands forth.
  Beneath the flighty maples, the blue
and bruiselike deeps of shade whisper a sad trifle,
    as if one were never to see them again
—or worse, would continue seeing them from this
    window only at this moment
for all of time, while the rest we had hoped to see
    —full of subtle change, free of complicity
—would break off, break up into a light puff of chalk
    or mass in tall chalk cliffs.

Off. Up. Out. From. Even those we love
    fly from us skirmishing
to get our attention
    as we gaze and gaze
at this dappling joyshow
    stretched out to the cisterns of purple
shadow through which a spider
    runs her streak of wet quick light.

These pretty things become so solid
    when we speak about them.
Like the dark and light of a mussel shell:
    —blue iris, mortal at their loveliest
too and the cut as well as the uncut
    grass equally evoking a sadness
as if the hotness of the evening it was
    made the heavy tears well up
from the throat, while the freshened midnight
    also emptied out the raw and already

exhausted eyes—until
      a handful of fireflies,
their musky neon spent,
      depart the dewy yard.

Moment, Stay

How to look away from what is painful?—
          —the stumbling of light   that
lapse   a faint slur
          of movement   at once keen
and cottony   nothing instant
          everything prolonged   drawn off . . .

To see the earwig
          touch the beard of pollen or water
dally along the passive
          sand, the moon   breathe   in its
ring of light—these
          as bitter
as actually to see
          teeth
rake across a vein.

Then: *therefore* is the bliss
          of holding what one loves
so hurry-hollow?

Because it is to meet
          in shape and
moisture and from

deep in the eye
          the features of
a ghost? To whom

do we say,

DO STAY,
FAIR BIRD?

Acting to Death

What one loves, what one hates, the swoon
recalled far after, the smile at midnight,
mind lithe at the center,
languorous orb in haze—

      —As soon as it regards itself, look
how haggard,
fretful, averse! Like dough
too much handled
(or the effort it must take to
act upon a stage): how wearisome always
to have to be
          doing something
with your body and your face—kneading
them into the   and the   and the
until the mind . . . the mind wants nothing more
to do with the antics
of the skeleton.

The eyes of the dark actor
fill the lids—haul up
the mask of will
(no longer taking in).

          Body,
of course, goes prattling on, sleek
and ripe
with designs,
but the heart's gone out.

Ladder of Sky

Profusion irksome
    all about her: however
    neatly she tries to move, each

limb knocks something over,
    a broken sprinkling of
    grit wherever she leans.

Rough too this
    seedcast of the mother
    in the child. And yet

stronger the trunk of somber
    mass that makes the world material
    amid the litter of assortment

as her years loom, uniform, than
    any program for the child.
    This is a forest clogged with hulls

she cannot make
    work, any longer. (Her wingèd
    dear another instance of

action without a use.) Precision-
    schooled, she therefore lacked
    "access to

the metaphysical world," Panofsky wrote
    —Yet she knows it's there, blue ladder
    above this zoo scene of inertia

matted like thorn and quickset in the tales.

      To flee, hold fast . . . like Beauty with her elbows
      on the granulated mortar

on the sill . . . and look out: There
      is the world in random miniature,
      tidy at a distance. Nuremberg.

The future with all its death.
      Could you rouse that life to
      order, nurse the child, force

to bloom dense bramble, do (to its end)
      the carpentry—would that then send
      a savior up the vine,

banish the spectral emanations
      like sheet lightning on the horizon? And when
      you felt your instep on the fiery transparent rung—

pierced through to that long climb
      of blue—*HUGE*—above this sluggish cloud
      the hue of tarnished copper—would that burnish

even gloom, the *true* blue
      with its dead surges of
      reluctance . . . mood indigo . . . ?

. . . Or leave it, a complexion
      foxed with sorrow,
      skittish discontent, flying

from tomorrow to this point? Was it
        gloom kept the hound, loose from the fruitless
        hunt, at best a haggard brute?

The Figure and Her Daughter

She is
a poor housekeeper yet one

who at one time made elegant
instruments, arrayed herself

adrift before the frame
with a wreath of cress

to counteract the dryness
of her essence. Not so

long ago on a crest of
self-mastery stiffening

as it grew, she hewed
the fantastic granite

ashlar into its fivefold faces,
employed the precision

compass on the mineral and metal
that mock her with a preatomic

stunned velocity; she though
can only pick

at the idle tip
of the silver compass

with her thumb. The slab
of stone crowned with

nothing is
heavy as heartache

while the radiant stone sphere
hovers near the rule with

no structure to adorn, no
flaring concave field of stars

to shine from—
monument to an altar

unfinishable and mocking
double of the great ball

of the fretful
figure's haunch

weighed down in a tangle
of sateen.

Flederzeug
(Bat Gear)

Here she will long sit. Perhaps the great stone
pentahedron will never sink into its niche. The scales
will gather dust. The sand half spent

in the shining hourglass
that seems to cramp
her great right wing

will run through
this last time then
cease to be stirred.

The seconds once
so finely sifted will
freak off, fanged and supersonic,

the fire in the tiny crucible wash out, the
lurid comet in the sky sink
(thank God), and the lunar bow

diminish into filaments of soul
like the gills on the meager hound
beached, just breathing.

Secondary Character

But the scribbling child, furious
feathered emblem of distraction
frowning at her writing—*what of her?*

Passionate, the infant imitates
the planet of slag
beside her, bent in some
desultory way

to arrest the mother
by roughing up this
offertory mayhem
on the tiny tablet

... loops and scrawls that do not speak
to the mother of the blues.

On her dangerous wheel
elate, uneasy,
the angel sees
her make
and mission:

What might *not*	*rumble up*
from the battered	*horizon*
if I	*were to stop*
gouging	*the tool*
at such a	*pitch*
into	*the slate ... ?*

If *she* stopped,
she would fall right to sleep,
dreaming of ink
to drink or stone
to soak it in, oblivious
to the allegory's
glory that required
          her fever
          for its fame.

La Nausée

Dark anger, Ruskin called it,
linked to labor with its deadly
grounding in the northern places
      where leisure is unlovely.

Ferocious dislocation of that work
in parts and pieces. Swarthy in the mounting
gall of a life half overcome by the too many
      objects of its universal study

daily returned to. Never the upsurge
of a strange idea but the extreme
of what already was discovered
      applied to what is capable of flaw.

Flame Lounge: The Night Behind the Day

Summer day in the cave of streets
nothing being worked
no ring
of apt hammer
on fresh board
or shaping
welcome even
should it bring
the shriek of bending
mineral

> only scrolls of noise
> from the machines
> of pleasure
> bass throb
> and idiot laughter
> from cars dealing
> in an alley

Granular look
of the breadth of sky
with night not all
diminished
chafing
to return

> the cries of
> mischief from
> children who rove
> urinating at will
> lifting
> rocks against large things

exploding
like tiny lightbulbs
going out
coming on
feverish in change
flickering in view

The car pulled up
and held itself in a dome
of unbroken red   no one got out
but there were others
behind the driver   nobody moved
no one got out
although the car was full
dark faces in profile   icons
of patience unmarred
for the moment
or were they
composing
their breath
for the jump

When he came the sheriff
sped backwards from the corner
to the full car
no one got out
perhaps some
            talking
passed between them

Had they been
traced to their silence
up all night
perspiring and taking
things in
creatures
who became themselves
only at night
angry to be torn
from the sharp shining
artifice of midnight the
long paths of speed

       Were they
       in this
       together
       or was one
       new to crime
       filling in for a brother
       paying down
       a father's debt

Were they fathers too
were their children roaming
through the alleys falling
into harm
       scarred
by desolation

       Did they even know
       their fathers

were they
     related
all the young men breathing
in their tank tops in the car
hands on their knees
in attitudes
of readiness

No
it turns out
a morning cut
from the same
thin piecework
as in the South
as summer in the train up
from the South
coal-smelling metal coaches
divaned in horsehair
cushions with a prickly nap
crusted with
dried food and fluid
of human drink and spew
in all the cracks and grooves
until even the tracks seem
worn
and snap with a spark
at every crossing
through a country
never sleeping
as if the depth

of all that
heat
       stored
in evening and
afternoon   one's own
or left by others
glowed deep
within the cushions
around restless heads
flicking from side to side
slowly
like horses' tails
all along the derelict
cored cities
clamped about
each tiny mountain
boxcars sprinkling rust
into a river already
low with sludge

Then the car emptied the five men
       their tall trunks moved
their faces large
       the rags of time
whipping
       along their torsos
through the slough
       of several hard
hours' hauling
       for the county

working against someone
    they
would not recognize
    on the street where
they dragged all
    her furniture   thinking
    If the sun went down
    would all this
    disappear

For once clear to see
through the window
in the door of the
car for some time
unopened
from which no young
black person
had as yet
unfolded himself
into the air
one of them
might have seen
breathing
a complete
ecocanopy
of green
within which
turned a dome
of darker green
till from it rang

birdsong
reverberant
with a sad
absorbed sound
as when wood
or earth
drinks down
to the clear
bottom of the
beaker
of silence
the bright
transferring clang
of iron
in a bell

> Or he might have heard
> smaller chimes
> sounding in the breeze
> also carrying the perfume
> of the tree Parajita
> amid the mordant
> howl and titter of
> temple monkeys
> high in the branches
> leopard splashed

Far down
    far off
in this scene
watchful creatures
would sound

as if their garden
hid an inner glen
only one
could find
when from the hold
he would pick
his way
to the deck
of the ship
in a bottle
where the clear drug
full of forgetting
beads
on the rigging

Hornbeam

Cendrillon, ou la petite pantoufle de verre
—CHARLES PERRAULT (*Contes du temps passé*, 1697)

Who was it, listening, when they got that wrong?
Not the slipper lined with FUR, but one of glass
—Obverse of animal—the rigid *verre*,
Cooling afterhusk of molten sand?

> *(Yet why was the young girl running*
> *out of it?)*

                       Wayward, did some
Slurry from the center of the tale
Pour off the heartsought
Hairy tenderness of the humble squirrel pelt
(Fuzzing around the often chilly feet)
Or more monarchic filaments of *vair*
No market maid could wear
Into the creepy nonsense homophone
Until the slipper hardened
Into glass
That only one foot fit?

Diminutive, reactive, almost hurtful

—*La petite pantoufle de verre*—

The slipper one could see through
Leaped out of the prince's ermine pocket
The moment he came down into the cloud
Of smell where she lay hid
Beneath a hornbeam tree.

Did they remember,
When they took dictation from the mouth
Of the old woman (Mother Ulmus,
Glossy as a nut, who'd gathered in
Around her dirty hearth those lazy,
Helpful animals of legend, turf croppers,
Myth cullers nibbling the blades over)—
Might they have been remembering, at her knee, as
Firelight gnawed self-consciously on heartwood,
The lozenges *vert* and *gules*
That posed a hart in branches
In the fanlight?

We're told which are the virtues
rewarded in the tales: presence
of mind, clear courage,
and that languid willingness
to take advice and be uncertainly
directed,
              but the rewards
were not transparent, always.
What of the white bird . . .

Was the young girl running
       out of it because
       —recall the blood
       within the shoe?—
       it hurt her?
       or else—
              or else—

Why has she fled
burying herself in the smoldering ash
with the potatoes for their meal? Is it
because the ring fit only her fine hand that once
fit on her mother's that she fled from *him* the while
her mother chirping from the hornbeam
would give her courage or,
by gazing above the jaw
(through the long eyes) of a
red calf, would
lean her disguise
into the little princess's
awareness or moving up
from the tame water
set
her finny head
which could not change expression
on the moss along the pond
where her daughter gazed . . . ?

(There's blood within the shoe)

little girl on the schoolbus amid the steel
glint of prosthesis and restraining bar
and (no doubt) the drool and babble of the other
damaged children; facing away
in her snow jacket and stocking cap, hands
without mittens (too cramped to draw cloth over them?)
waving from the hinge
of the wrist in a short, grinding

flitch that keeps on taking her
knuckles against the window . . .
long repetitions of the tiny mystery
(or meaningless refrain): would she be sore,
or barely conscious of it by this time?

But where among the clusters of light green nuts in that true place is the
white bird sitting on the hazel twig, with her brimming heifer's eyes, who
waited there with her daughter until the wickedness ran out and the child
grew one with the world she looked upon, with no tremor intervening, or
fitful visitation from the delusional plane, or convulsion of voices bidding
her upon pain of her life to dress in the worst rags and draw across her form
the caul of cinders and deformity, her menial sluttishness a kind of cramp
in the greater spirit she was born to be, the dirt stuck fast to her face and
skin, an attitude of powerless dread in the bones—never to let others see her
in the clear . . . a beauty at the edge of movement, alive, supple, still . . . ?

Mother Mimulus

Mother Nummularium

Mother Holle

Mother Ilex

birch   ironwood   hornbeam   polished deal

plant and inexhaustible mineral

sad, helpful animals

and meteor magic,

firefolk sitting in the air, fire-featured

Why was the young girl running
        although her heart
        her tiny tender self
        told her to savor
the candelabrum glancing off the mirror
        above her image
as she breathed out against the streaks
of silver dimpling down the gown?

        Did her heart also
        whisper her to flee
back to the midden and the servile mask
of ashes and punishing work
like hauling water under a yoke
        or picking lentils
        (they might as well be tears)
        from the oily embers?
Why bear this rude disguise that made her name
        ("Rashin Coatie,"
        Smock of Rushes)
        anything but happy?

"My heart is good,
But I am still a monster, don't forget."
This is what the little beauty heard,
"Don't forget, or *do:* I am a beast,
But oh, my thought is air."

Toxic Songs

Then all at once in Carbonek
A red pawn on the board moved
Forward by itself.

Dozens of hands lit dozens of candles and dozens reached
Wine to his arms. "My heart of course
Is good, but still I am

a monster—see how the tooth

grows, how the itch

smokes in my hide

(which to resist is thirst
more fierce than I can bear)—
I'd have given in
except a vow had kept me silent
allein ein Schwur
drückt mir die Lippen zu ..."

All lyric from the depths. The poems glitter
With the sadness that is joy, though some are
Tugged back from the edge by drugs
Named with a crazed flair out of William Blake
(Luvah? Palamabron? Urizen?):
Luvox, Porpramin, Prolixin—or worse, like cyber
Villains wearing tights and ruff (Effexor,
Zoloft, Nardil, Ativan—which counteracts
The sense
Of doom):

Une triste boutique—*a weary business, living,*
which we must brighten, says Flaubert, with guile.

Then when the patient
Funks all other
Remedies, the toxic jewel
Of the dark with moth-wing eyes
And studded nails,
Clozaril,
Death on her further side . . . This is the night
With no beginning

The Star Lantern

All day the hoary meteor, black Boreas, deadly Electric
Streams in the firmament, furious with despair, like the Lions
Of burning gas or the other stars, themselves
Destroyers in outlandish patterns of Lethean
Pool and Scimitar and Vug the cavern
Lined with crystals flashing quartz-fret
Or sparks of salt. In those days seeking
Death, not finding it, death fleeing on
Before, although you were promised, later, you might find him
In Arcadia, too, at dawn in a crust of stars, the brightest
One called Wormwood going and coming in the curve of nature,
The warp of the sphere, as Hopkins called it, which the falling
Stars always seem to wish to imitate, stars
That wore the habit
Of insatiable desire.

Percivale the blank babe who cannot understand the woodland music
Of the armor jingling as two knights ride through the unnamed trees,
Royal princeling with a toy who, having killed, does not know how
The red knight's cuirass works and so cannot take it off.
(Out of the iron burn the tree, the woodsman hinted.) Percivale is found
Brooding when the eagle kills the dove;
When he has visited the Wye; when recognizing the lady Blanchefleur
Wearing his token. The knight of silences, like the small
Egyptian god Harpocrates. Combing through
Wordless dreck piled up at the chimney's back,
Rubbish of memory mounting behind the firescreen of his seizures . . .
The places he kept walking to were empty, not even weeds would grow
Between the disenchanted slates.

Burn the wood, boil the body, use the
Sun method, the method of boiling—or steeping in
Rock-water for too great a tendency
To self-reproach, too rigid a self-discipline;
Gorse, whin, or furze for very great hopelessness,
Crab apple if you feel unclean,
Holly for envy,

                hornbeam

Should you fear you haven't strength
Daily to rise and repeat yourself
In work. And for those who hide
Beneath a face of cheer
Their worst discouragement and desperate
Gloom (for which no explanation can be given),
Gentian   felwort   mustard   agrimony
Take these so the smiling mask
May loosen and the twist of pain
Relapse into its writhing;
Star of Bethlehem for shock . . .
Cherry-plum in case of fear the mind
May give way . . . But retain
Red chestnut for that worst
Of fears, anxiety for others, agapê.

        How different is day
Fire—antidote to will,
Back cloth for the starry flake and pellicle.
Agrippa the physician thought wood
Fires augmented
The bright work of the light
Bearing angels to chase off demons
Into the unmeaning beat of

Ghostly fingertips of sleet
Beneath a great heartblinding ball
With blackness bound, the plough all
Golden falling, Cassiopeia on end with her bright
Quains, Perseus beneath her. More
Meteor magic from Parnassus.

Pavel Isaev, Dostoevsky's stepson, falling to his death
From the steep tower knew everything
Broken, the writer's make
And ghost, who must have seen
Something—
Electrons
—Tossed out in a cloud
In the silence, his mind
Untried, flowering into abstract
Rivers of articulation.

Chattanooga dying alongside the ruined river
The mountains with their knees drawn up
Weep frozen tears to the oily current
Of the Tennessee, ankles
Manacled to the spent mills
Of earth like Orc
In flames of change or
Floods of horror

We built by rivers and at night the water
Running past our windows comforted our sorrow
The sorrow cast across our lives by mountains

Sad songs in the night, not made by god
Only by water around the lifeless stone

Even the round moon scarred
And the stars, not clean

But the rain comes down
And brings—not depression,
No—*elation,* a thrill of
The absolute: the Nothing
That has yet to form itself
Out of the veering spiral
Where the rain drives, not
Falling, but coursing and
Swiveling its pepper pattern
On the water and also changing
The lurid brunt of air
As if, off in the sky, a
Nodule of ink had opened,
Tainting the air a green
So dark the black
It slithered into
Grew a minute
After-sheen, and in
This somber
Vortex the truth
Of your being
Welling up could
Whisper like *La Belle*
Au bois dormant or the jetcraft
When the red line falls

Past zero as if elements
Were being torn then
Recomposed
Till one speck held itself
Intact momentarily
In a blare of schematic
Stuff collapsing, bombarded,
Reforming like
Technetium in the chamber
And you saw there—
Yes, it was!—the glowing
Stone—one you could feel
Like a warm patch in the
Icy floor, telling you
That what you wanted
Was near, and that it was
Right, to live.

Drift

We call out to each other from adjacent rooms.
I hear the rasp that carries through the wall,

Mama I'm cold

Trickle of water wearing away at a stone

What if I should die?
And not be able to tell
Her how to save herself,
What sort of call to make
In the morning? With what
Demeanor to proceed about
Her feeling for me now
That I am gone? (It should be
Practical, but on occasion tender.)

Wait. Don't let me go yet.
(To whom do I say that?)

Who was
That woman in France with twins and a student lover
Whose children were brought up like strangers though
They found a way, like Pyramus and Thisbe, to pierce
Through all her hardness, by obeying the inverse
Way, the via negativa, speech through silence,
Talking only through a wall, praising her permission
And the need to seek it just to leave
Their rooms, when need be
Appalling her that they could live

Only on the message of that breath
That came and went in both their breasts
The same . . .
                    To show her how the silence
Risen up from their hard beds in truth
Was eloquence
To one another, the outward crown
Of rings fleeting away in water, single
Teardrops made by tiny objects in a now
Familiar and beloved vacancy,
All the absence a close concentric weft of
Circles in time named and particular
That must keep crossing the other
Mandalas of water, arc
Caressing arc of solace
In the abstract,
Only to her senses
Empty.

                    Found at last alive
By others after she
Had killed herself for love—leading that second
Life in a kind of panic parting from them—
The pantry empty, the fire gone cold,
The children would only answer
What they were asked, but not come out
Of the little nests of their imprisonment.

                            I still hear them,
Trickles of icy water whispering comfort to each other
Wordless through a wall, their future lives

Thinning tufts of flame
Before the tomb of their real lives—
The past, those hours inching
Through the afternoon of childhood
Sometimes filled only
By stalactites
Of time dripping.
                                   Are we too

Stalled here in some fruitless
Honeycomb of pattern
Celled by separation?

Sunk down so far in half sleep I cannot
Get up
Cross the hall
Pursue the conversation—

        Well try to take some covers off, I say,

Which she forgets by morning anyway—
            In fact, she is asleep
            Even as we speak.

After Frost at Midnight

Heard only in the trances of the blast
—SAMUEL TAYLOR COLERIDGE

     Moonrise, and no one wakened to notice how
     Savage or hard the trances can sound from here
          Where light picks out the deeper patches
        Darkened by wind as if wind were knowledge.

     Scraps rustle, stuck to a frozen canal where in
     Summer, or later, there would be fragrances
          Moved upward, felt by us as living,
        Mingled with flecks of the chimney vapor.

     Easy to think the cosmos grows poisonous
     Or worse, while we improve: individuals
          Marked out, despite our forlorn virtue
        Eagerly wishing for nothing over.

Zeno at Zero

The skin, at first like dust, began to loose
The torment of the flesh to airiness,
All his body's bounds from their duress
Relinquished. A reluctant and diffuse
Grace attends this as if the long fuss
Of waiting were no trial, the dinginess
Swarmed out upon his dying powerless
Against his scorn's degrading animus.

He had no life to speak of, no career
After the first depressions, waiting out
The world's compulsive exercise of skill
And constant, low-pitched bragging. His one fear,
That he would seem a supplicant. No doubt
He lasted as he did by rage of will.

The Harriers

He hardly ever used the telephone
Except to dial and listen to the weather,
Or utter something recordlike,
Handling at a distance some affair.

It was a quiet winter. Their talk, so soft
It drifted through the registers to fade
In an occasional bright ring of pans or the stubborn
Thrust of hand into a stiff glove.

The phone rang into silence like God's voice
With whom they dealt

                       meek and watchful—

Until a deaf and angry myriad began
To put calls through, whom nothing but
Verbatim repetition pacified
At thunderous volume.

Shaken by their worst
At its loudest
She trembled at his undulating whisper
As between bells it palpably
Retreated into the dry cave.

Looking In at Night

Asleep, alive, her shape makes me afraid.
Afraid to lose what lasts a little while—
A curl of light along her shoulder blade,

One elbow up but the round ear in shade,
Mouth serious, eyes inward in denial
Of waking life—her shape makes me afraid.

She is like a statue they've displayed,
A maiden's (from the porch), with her unseeing smile.
Light is sketched along her shoulder blade

And weaves around her head like waves of braid,
Suggesting hair in an archaic style,
Asleep-alive. Her shape makes me afraid,

Every year the marble more decayed,
The lines less clear. Time starts its slide,
Curling the light along her shoulder blade

Then rubbing out the features we have made
To take the wing and numbers from the dial.
Alive in sleep her shape turns, unafraid,
Drawing the night along her shoulder blade.

Objet

Dear child, why
is it still, along the pillow
this hand of yours half
open on the brightness
thrown by the lamp
anemone in
water the current
once passed through

In sleep you answer
that life catches
against the edge of
its own likeness
vein ever blue
in the body's
marble drift

NOTE

Flame Lounge was the name of a rough jazz club on Chicago's near south side in the 1950s. The poet William Hunt says, "The Flame Lounge was in a neighborhood that no one would be safe entering, unless they were themselves among those who preyed on others."

A NOTE ABOUT THE AUTHOR

Mary Kinzie is the author of *A Poet's Guide to Poetry* and five earlier collections of poetry, including *Summers of Vietnam, Autumn Eros*, and *Ghost Ship*. She teaches in the creative writing program she founded two decades ago at Northwestern University.

A NOTE ON THE TYPE

This book was set in a typeface called Walbaum. The original cutting of this face was made by Justus Erich Walbaum (1768–1839) in Weimar in 1810. The type was revived by the Monotype Corporation in 1934. Young Walbaum began his artistic career as an apprentice to a maker of cookie molds. How he managed to leave this field and become a successful punch cutter remains a mystery. Although the type that bears his name may be classified as modern, numerous slight irregularities in its cut give this face its humane manner.

Composed by MD Linocomp
Westminster, Maryland

Printed and bound by United Book Press
Baltimore, Maryland

Designed by Soonyoung Kwon